EXECUTIVE BRIEFING:

P.E.O.P.L.E. GOALS

*Six leadership tips to guide your
organization to success*

EXECUTIVE BRIEFING:

P.E.O.P.L.E. GOALS

*Six leadership tips to guide your
organization to success*

PAM WESTON

Progress Partners
P.O. Box 146, Belleville, IL 62221 -1111

ISBN: 978-0-9600187-0-3

Library of Congress Control Number: 2018965047

Edited by Shelia E. Bell sheliawritesbooks@yahoo.com

Printed In United States of America

Praise for Executive Briefing: P.E.O.P.L.E. Goals

"*Executive Briefing: P.E.O.P.L.E. Goals* is filled with great examples and practical tips to help us along the journey to intentional leadership. This is a perfect guide for leaders."
-JEFF VONDEYLEN, CEO Ensono

"Pam Weston provides a brilliant tutorial for reminding leaders what matters most in building a business and taking care of your clients...P.E.O.P.L.E. Failure to make people a priority can undermine your innovation, stifle growth, and slowly erode your business. She captures the essence of managing the keys to our success...our employees and leaders."
-DANN ADAMS, President, Equifax Global Consumer Services

"Having worked in corporate America for over 40 years, with most of my career spent in Human Resources, I found this book quite informative, interesting, easy to follow, and much needed by business people in all stages of their careers."
-SHELIA E. BELL, Author and former HR compensation analyst/administrative professional

DEDICATION

To my mother, for instilling the will to do more
To Rose, for encouraging me to do more

TABLE OF CONTENTS

INTRODUCTION
P.E.O.P.L.E. GOALS

Employee advocate, Natalie Carlsen, graduated twenty years ago from a prestigious university after completing internships with firms in several industries and in multiple concentrations within Finance. Since her senior year in high school, she worked to position herself as a quality candidate in an increasingly competitive job market. She recalled her father sharing stories from his thirty-five-year career. His tales of working hard at a company with leaders who respected his talents and who encouraged him to grow as an individual is what Natalie wanted to experience.

Unlike her father, Natalie's career journey was filled with deviations due to mergers, market shifts, and acquisitions. She also encountered a series of leaders who missed the mark on creating an environment that nurtured the best in people while engaging them to achieve mutual goals. Many who occupied the C-Suites[1] in companies where she worked over the years failed to realize the importance of focusing on employees, in addition to the bottom line.

Many times, individuals are promoted to management roles based on their expertise in a job function. Just as often, this new position includes the responsibility of leading others. Frequently, new managers are not prepared or capable of effectively leading others. As a result, subordinates suffer through poor leadership or leave the organization.

Natalie leads a successful, midsized accounting firm. She is in tune with her team and what is required of her for the team, and her, to continue to win. She has done the work as an executive to shift her mindset to one that values people. Her leadership team gets it too. Together, they are shaping an environment where employees show up with purpose, engage in their jobs, and feel

---

[1] The highest-level executives in senior management usually with titles beginning with "chief".

empowered to perform.

Getting to this level of leadership requires a shift in how people are viewed. Employees are the link to your company's success. They are your most valuable asset and should feel this when they show up for work every day. This is easier for some in the C-Suite and can take more time for others. It also takes effort. You must be intentional in your approach to making this an employee reality.

It starts with P.E.O.P.L.E. (Prioritize, Engage, Originate, Persevere, Lead, Execute). Your team must be just as important to you as hitting revenue targets. After all, you need each employee to help achieve those goals. It is satisfying to achieve your financial goals each quarter. Make it a priority to exceed your P.E.O.P.L.E. goals too.

As the saying goes, perception is reality. In your position, you should want to know what employee perceptions are shaping their reality in the workplace. The employee reality must be at the center of every C-Suite leader's business plan.

You want to retain good people, engage employees, and produce value for the business. This requires getting involved beyond the corner office and leading throughout your organization. Active involvement from senior executives in shaping the employee reality leads to desired universal perceptions. Traditional ways that companies seek to attract and retain employees, which include benefits, compensation, flexible hours, and paid time off are all great. What is missing from this are P.E.O.P.L.E. goals.

The heart of the employee experience starts with people. It is true: when employees have great interactions at work, it translates to satisfied customers and better results for the business.

Focusing on the employee reality is generally delegated to a team of people in human resources or organizational development. I am not debating where this task should sit within an organization. I want to stress that the C-Suite should drive the focus on the employee reality and the organizational culture.

4

It takes the *right leader* implementing the *right actions* to influence the *right behavior.* Set your P.E.O.P.L.E. goals today!

CHAPTER 1

PRIORITIZE

pri·or·i·tize \ prī-'ȯr-ə-ˌtīz, -'är-; 'prī-ə-rə- \ *verb*
1: to organize (things) so that the most important thing
is done or dealt with first

**Ensuring employees know *why* translates into
purposeful actions.** Patricia does things right. She
knows that people matter. However, several
members of her leadership team operate
differently. It became clear to her during regular
chats and visits with employees across the company
that many were not feeling included.

Although annual performance reviews and mid-
year reviews were in place, Patricia decided it was
worth implementing a pulse check[2] to address
employee concerns. She scheduled a meeting with
human resources and organizational development

---

[2] Method used to determine the attitude or temperament of your group.

to share her observations. Her direct reports were also invited to the meeting. Patricia charged them with creating a structured assessment that could be implemented systemwide within the next three months. The goal was to assess how connected employees were to their leaders and teams. Patricia also wanted to understand how employees were contributing to the strategy.

Representatives from human resources and organizational development were identified to lead the process that included planned updates to Patricia and her team. Leaders were able to use the data to highlight departments that were well connected to the strategy. They also identified teams that were not in the loop due to lack of engagement, poor management performance, and lack of clarity from leaders.

Priorities: A $185 million Culture Problem

A culture that prioritizes people first allows employees to thrive along the path toward organizational success. In business, we have seen where some employee actions are the result of an

7

entrenched culture that rewards deceitful behavior for the sake of increased profits at the expense of the team. In one such case, the Consumer Finance Protection Bureau fined Wells Fargo $185 million in 2016 due to fraudulent sales practices involving creating millions of fake savings and checking accounts on behalf of clients without their consent. Investigators estimated 1.5 million illegal accounts were opened.

How a leader responds can often reveal whether the crisis is the result of a situation or a systemic culture problem. Your employees are equally concerned about how their company and leaders are perceived in the public. How well you perform could have a lasting impact. Initially, the former CEO, John Stumpf, communicated that the fraud was a result of sales practices and not indicative of its culture and strategic plan. This was found to be otherwise as employees reported they were pressured to generate sales despite unreasonable and at times impossible quotas which led to a culture of unethical and illegal behavior across the organization.

Over time, and with new leadership, the company has an opportunity to rebuild the culture from a perspective that positions employees to excel. Focused investments in teams, along with targeted training and aligned resources, would help the company move forward. Leaders operating with this mindset realize that investing in people is what leads to the business achieving its bottom line. It is imperative to drive this behavior across the organization. To do that, leaders have to work systemwide to know their clients better, build solutions that meet their needs, and anticipate future opportunities.

LEADER TIP

Keep the drive alive in everyone. Challenge yourself to communicate to employees beyond your direct reports. This also means demanding accountability throughout your organization by people leaders.

Make people a priority. Think about it...if an employee does not feel like they have a purpose then what is their motivation for showing up daily?

As the leader of the organization, your purpose is clear. You are driven to ensure profitability, shareholder returns, and continued growth for the business. Your decisions are designed to move goals forward each quarter.

Your business may be performing well, but what about your people. What is driving your team? Do employees know why they are asked to perform certain tasks? Will you lose good people within one-to-three-years because they do not feel like you care? This should be important to you as a leader, especially for future success.

Just like you, employees must have the information they need to perform and respond better. Knowing how their work contributes to the organization can increase purpose, participation, and profits.

Vision starts at the top, but it does not end there. You, along with senior leaders, must make employees a priority and not an afterthought. Imagine the kind of results your company could experience when employees know why they show up every day.

PAM WESTON

ACT NOW

Ensuring employees know why translates into purposeful actions.

How will you prioritize to ensure that employees know their purpose and drive their actions toward common business goals?

_____

_____

_____

_____

_____

_____

_____

_____

_____

_____

_____

_____

_____

_____

_____

_____

_____

_____

CHAPTER 2

ENGAGE

en·gage \ in-'gāj, en- \ *verb*

1: to hold the attention of

**If you want employees to be engaged, you
must be connected.** Emory was successful at
checking the list on ways to engage with employees.
What he missed was valuing the process, hearing
from employees, and acting on feedback.

Employees repeatedly provided feedback that
they wanted to hear more about how the work they
did every day contributed to the success of the
organization. What they continued to hear instead
in each town hall, quarterly update, and leadership
roundtable was more about the bottom line and
cold, hard numbers. Sure, they enjoyed his visits to
their sites, but when he left, they were no more

connected on how to meet those numbers than before he came.

Most leaders believe in data. When Emory was presented with a compilation of the direct quotes and feedback that employees from several locations provided after meeting with him, it became clear to him that employees need to hear more than the numbers.

Developing a way to assess the many employee encounters was the first step. Next, following up to share the data with leaders took the process further. As a leader, being open to hearing voices besides your own aids in positioning you to connect and hold your team's attention. Emory challenged his team to follow his lead and push this process throughout the organization.

Dangerous Engagement

Sometimes, leaders are faced with circumstances where it is not about proving your organization was without fault. It is about engaging in a way that shows remorse and a commitment to improve the situation.

In 2010, one of the largest industrial disasters occurred when The Deepwater Horizon oil drilling rig owned by Transocean and leased by BP exploded in the Gulf of Mexico, causing oil to leak for five months.

This disaster caused 11 deaths and 17 injuries, with many more experiencing long-term effects from the oil leak and the solvent used to clean up the spill. Investigators reported increased loss among marine life in the areas where the oil leaked and traveled. Ultimately, BP agreed to pay more than $18 billion in fines related to this incident.

Tony Hayward was the CEO at BP during this time. With each response, he created a deeper divide between BP, the public, and those directly impacted by this tragic accident. He was seen as being tone-deaf as he repeatedly denied BP's responsibility and minimized the magnitude of the impact in press interviews. Hayward was eventually replaced as the leader for the oil spill response and as CEO.

Ideally, the company would have led with a sympathetic and honest approach in its initial response. While this was not the case, BP leadership could have redirected its CEO's engagement with the public and the media in subsequent messaging.

As a leader, it is essential to connect with stakeholders. Just as it is important to capture the passion of employees to motivate them in their roles, the same concept is true when communicating outside the organization. When the public is alienated and does not feel engaged, stakeholders are not accepting of you as a leader and any messages that are shared.

LEADER TIP

Get to know what you do not know. Find out what is really going on. Focus on managers with responsibility for leading others.

Stop and ask the question...Am I connected? As the leader, your words and actions can be more powerful when you are directing a workforce that feels connected. Engagement requires listening, hearing, and acting on what employees value.

One of your primary goals must be capturing the passion of employees and liberating it into processes, teamwork, and leadership. Translating passion into positive results makes the difference in an engaged workforce.

Encourage other people leaders to build personal relationships on their teams and across the organization. Connecting with employees and sustaining that engagement is key to transforming a workforce. Engagement is a two-way process. In order to initiate, nurture, and sustain a productive connection to employees, leaders must be open to the truth of what matters to people.

Take it one or two steps further and hold people leaders accountable for employee engagement. Insist on structured training and development that will allow them to grow as leaders in how they motivate, develop, and relate to their teams.

ACT NOW

If you want employees to be engaged, you must be connected.

How will you ensure employees are engaged and connected to the goals of your organization?

_____

_____

_____

_____

_____

_____

_____

_____

_____

_____

_____

_____

_____

_____

_____

_____

_____

CHAPTER 3

ORIGINATE

orig·i·nate \ ə-ˈri-jə-ˌnāt \ *verb*

1: to begin to exist: to be produced or created

Create an atmosphere that empowers innovation without limitations. If there was one thing that Oscar believed in, it was exemplifying the company's values. After all, he was a third-generation CEO of the corporation his grandfather founded. It was important to him to carry on his family's legacy and sustain the business for the next generations.

A master branding expert, Oscar realized staying the course could, at times, result in undesired results.

Oscar took the initiative to ensure the founding values were in place across the organization. He also went further to evaluate whether the principles

20

in writing were still right for the 90-year-old firm. While it was personal for him, it was also a priority for the business that employees experienced what the company promoted to customers.

Oscar was in search of what still made their employees excited about being on the team and whether adjustments were needed. While the company performed well, he also wanted everyone to experience and treasure what was original for the organization.

Propelled into Something New

You are at the forefront of managing internal operations as well as external events that may lead to scrutiny. A classic crisis management case in business as well as academia is how Johnson & Johnson responded to the first known case of deliberate product tampering in Chicago in 1982. Investigators never determined who was responsible for lacing Extra Strength Tylenol capsules with potassium cyanide poison, resulting in seven deaths.

James Burke, CEO, made protecting people the company's priority during this incident. The company immediately removed 31 million bottles of Tylenol, valued at $100 million, off the shelves and halted manufacturing and advertising of the product.

During this process, Burke and his team developed a model for responding to a crisis, and communicating openly became a blueprint for other corporations. He was commended for establishing partnerships with the Chicago Police, FBI, and FDA to ensure the public remained informed throughout the investigation.

As the leader of Johnson & Johnson, Burke was expected to reduce the impact of financial loss. However, his strategy and communications to the public focused on putting people first. He prioritized the most important element in this situation, which was to inform people to help them make the best decisions for protecting themselves. Johnson & Johnson's market share suffered initially, but rebounded in less than a year.

Additionally, the company originated in other ways by introducing the first tamper-resistant packaging when the capsules were reintroduced to consumers.

LEADER TIP

Proactively inspire your team. Avoid the cookie-cutter approach to addressing organizational issues.

You know what distinguishes your business from your competitors, but what about internally? Is this a place where employees are excited about working? Do potential employees view your organizational culture as one where they want to grow their careers? Your products, service, and innovation set you apart and so should the way you interact with your people.

You have an opportunity to create an organizational culture that complements your external strategy for marketing your business. Be original and innovative in setting the tone for shaping the employee reality.

Seek to understand whether the company's core values are truly what employees experience daily while working on projects, in teams, and interacting with their managers. Are you, your direct reports, and other people leaders producing the best experiences for your people?

Each organization is unique. The approach to transforming it into one where employees are connecting and performing at high levels takes work.

ACT NOW

Create an atmosphere that empowers
innovation without limitations.

*How will you drive innovation in a way that
connects with employees and propels your
organization forward?*

_____

_____

_____

_____

_____

_____

_____

_____

_____

_____

_____

_____

_____

_____

CHAPTER 4

PERSEVERE

persevere \ pər-sə-ˈvir\ *verb*
1: to persist in a state, enterprise, or undertaking despite counterinfluences, opposition, or discouragement

Cultivating a good organizational culture requires perseverance. Leaders face staff changes, acquisitions, plant closings, innovation, and more. While Pilar was set to retire in 18 months due to a mandatory retirement policy, she stayed engaged to move the business forward. During her tenure, she enjoyed years of dominating the market with new products and the accolades that came as a result of her leadership.

This year, the outlook was different and taking a toll on the company's financial goals. Pilar could have easily transitioned and allowed the incoming leader to get the company out of this uncharacteristic downfall of low profits and dejected employees.

Pilar was well aware that what the business was experiencing was negatively impacting the team's morale. She was also clear that it may take more than two years to see the change everyone needed. Despite seeming to have time working against her, Pilar persevered and led the organization as she had in previous years. She made it a priority to keep employees at the center of the plan toward turning the company around.

Stay the Course

Pushing through in the face of a crisis can be a true test of leadership. Airlines have had their share of public lashings due to unintended circumstances. One of the largest was Southwest Airlines' technology outage in the summer of 2017 that halted flights across the carrier's entire system in the United States. A faulty router shut down the computer network for 12 hours, resulting in 2,300 delayed flights over five days.

Southwest's leadership knew they were facing a situation where it would take some time to determine the cause of the outage. They were also mindful to provide a timely response to console customers impacted by the outage. The first response from Southwest was to engage with its customers to apologize and offer options for rebooking and refunds.

The team persevered and communicated what they knew at the moment while working on a solution. Southwest's Chief Operating Officer, Michael Van de Ven, led the way and issued a video apology via the company's Facebook page. In addition to providing an update on what his team had done so far to resolve the issue, he provided answers to questions customers posted on its corporate Facebook and Twitter sites. By expressing sympathy and focusing his messaging on what customers needed, Van de Ven was able to engage them with his message and future updates until the airline was fully functional.

LEADER TIP

Challenge leaders to make shaping the employee reality a priority and stick to it.

Your organization may be in varying stages toward attaining an employee reality that produces the desired results.

As companies and industries evolve, leaders must be determined to make hard decisions for the good of the organization. Your goal is to provide employees with an atmosphere that inspires engagement and ultimately boosts the bottom line.

People matter and should be at the center of what inspires leaders to push through. Crafting a plan and identifying points of progress along the way will help guide your team through the stages of growth, setbacks, breakthroughs, and success.

Just as leadership shifts tactics as teams, markets, and industries evolve, it is important to adjust to improve the organizational culture to remain competitive.

ACT NOW

Cultivating a good organizational culture requires perseverance.

How will you lead your organization toward attaining milestones on specific culture initiatives that may be taking longer to achieve?

_____

_____

_____

_____

_____

_____

_____

_____

_____

_____

_____

_____

_____

_____

_____

_____

CHAPTER 5

LEAD

\ 'lēd \ *verb*

1: to direct the operations, activity, or performance of

Set the stage for leadership and invite your team to play. After forming her leadership team and giving the directive for a multi-year strategy, Lyn was focused on the end game. This was despite direct reports leaving for other opportunities within and outside of the organization. She also heard of demoralizing behavior of some direct reports that remained on the senior leadership team. It was clear to everyone, except Lyn, that self-reflection and a reality check was needed to correct behaviors and engage employees.

A 360-degree performance review[3] of Lyn's leadership style and behavior conducted by an outside consultant would help her understand the depth of the issues on her immediate team. Focus groups among employees impacted by the adverse behavior of her direct reports and the employees whose leaders had recently left the company would provide additional insight.

Taking steps to acknowledge and address behaviors that impact employee engagement and productivity requires real leadership. Remaining objective and open without punishing employees for providing feedback is crucial to successfully moving the team forward during the process.

Now that you have the data, what are you going to do with it? Be honest and transparent in developing a plan to modify your own behavior. Set new expectations for leadership, while providing coaching and mentoring to keep people leaders on

---

[3] Process used to obtain feedback from employee's subordinates, colleagues, and supervisor, as well as a self-evaluation by the employee

track.

Stop, Regulate, and Listen

You will be required to pause and evaluate conditions beyond the corner office, even though from your perspective, the company is moving ahead as planned. Prior to complaints related to a 2010 recall of nearly 9 million vehicles, Toyota was known for producing quality products. Customers reported issues related to sudden acceleration, including multiple injuries and 89 deaths.

Initially, the leadership team took a reactive approach to addressing the problem. In response to customer complaints, Toyota communicated a number of reasons for the malfunctions, including operator error, floor mats, and sticky gas pedals. This approach significantly impacted Toyota's bottom line and market position.

Jim Lentz, president and chief operating officer, appeared on a national morning news program in an underwhelming performance. Immediately after the interview, customers criticized Lentz for evading facts that were presented by the reporter indicating Toyota was aware of the problem prior to the current crisis. Additionally, Akio Toyoda, chief executive, endured contentious congressional hearings.

As time passed, the company publicly accepted responsibility. An independent study found no electronic flaws in Toyota vehicles that could lead to the acceleration issues. Since this recall, the company has regained the public's trust, increased market position, and continues to be known for its commitment to quality.

We can all agree that leaders set the tone for how a corporation performs, including what behavior is perceived as acceptable. While organizations may experience uncomfortable situations internally or externally, leaders are charged with stepping up in these times.

Internal documents showed Toyota was previously aware of data related to the 2010 recall, however, did not act appropriately to prevent future problems. These are scenarios where a good leader must pause to regulate nonproductive behavior. This includes a self-analysis to ensure that her or his actions are not sending the message that it is okay to behave, communicate, and approach their jobs a certain way.

LEADER TIP

Model the behavior that other leaders should embrace, and set expectations for leadership.

You are the key to shaping the atmosphere that permeates throughout your firm. Leaders do as their leaders do. The behavior that you allow is a direct reflection of your character and management style. Self-reflection provides a chance for you to regulate nonproductive behaviors. This also allows you to execute the beliefs, behaviors, and processes that promote a healthy culture.

Do a reality check. If you have people leaders exhibiting behaviors that do not inspire their teams to perform, address it immediately. The worse thing to do is ignore it and allow one or two individuals to become the norm in your business.

ACT NOW

Set the stage for leadership and invite your team to play.

How will you demand accountability from yourself and all people leaders within your organization?

_____

_____

_____

_____

_____

_____

_____

_____

_____

_____

_____

_____

_____

_____

_____

_____

_____

CHAPTER 6

Execute

execute \ 'ek-si-‚kyüt \ *verb*

1: to carry out fully: put completely into effect

Provide employees with the right information to help them perform and respond better. Throughout her career in sales, Elisabeth had a great reputation for closing the deal. She could quickly bring clarity to any situation and engage others around mutual points. She was also known for her charisma and connecting with employees at all levels to achieve business goals. As Elisabeth advanced in her career, she continued to hone these skills and grow as a business leader.

After years of relocating to various states and two countries, everything seemed to align for Elisabeth. She was offered an opportunity to move her family back to her hometown as the CEO of a major distribution corporation. Elisabeth was recruited for her ability to lead people and improve profits consistently for a number of companies.

At the heart of what allowed Elisabeth to be successful for so many years was her philosophy to proactively design opportunities to connect with team members. She became proficient at prioritizing the people within the organizations she led. Consistently engaging in a way that clearly communicated the vision and the contributions for each department was important to Elisabeth. Each time she stepped into a new role, she assessed what would work best for the respective employees and the business. Elisabeth was a born leader and continually examined how her actions influenced her team and the entire business. She also mentored others with the goal of providing employees with a reality that aligned with the company's values.

Empowered to Deescalate

Empowering people to execute can help pivot your team and firm to the next level. Think about what can happen when employees are not empowered. As an employee advocate, you want your entire team to be fully engaged and able to execute in a way that propels the company forward.

In 1987, a lit match was unintentionally dropped into an escalator starting a fire at the King's Cross station of the London Underground rapid transit system. Tragically, 31 people died and 1,000 were injured. The burning wooden escalator produced heated gases that rose to the top of its ceiling, which were absorbed by layers of old paint and contributed to the intensity of the fire as it spread.

After several investigations to confirm the cause, new fire safety regulations were developed. Wooden escalators were phased out in exchange for metal ones. Additionally, members of the senior management team at the London Underground resigned as a result of this catastrophe. You can

41

imagine that a transit system requires a multitude of workers with specific responsibilities to maintain operations. Were they empowered to execute for the best interest of the organization and the people they served?

During the investigation, it was revealed that the director of external operations informed his colleagues that the buildup of paint on the ceiling of the escalator shaft could become hazardous. His concerns were ignored because rules related to painting were not in the scope of his job. No precautions were taken to remove 20 years' worth of paint to potentially prevent a serious public safety problem. This employee was not able to fully execute because he was not empowered by leaders to make meaningful decisions and champion fearlessness.

LEADER TIP

Lead clearly and consistently.

Results matter. This means that like you, all employees should be focused on growing your business and achieving your results.

Working with your leadership team, design the right strategies to ensure that all employees are connected to solve your business needs.

As the employee advocate and leader of your organization, provide direction that consciously creates opportunities to connect employees to the vision.

Direct the right people to lead initiatives and demand open communications. Empower leaders to make meaningful decisions. Champion fearlessness.

ACT NOW

Provide employees with the right information to help them perform and respond better.

How will you ensure that employees are collectively working on the right things to produce the best results for your organization?

_____

_____

_____

_____

_____

_____

_____

_____

_____

_____

_____

_____

_____

_____

_____

_____

_____

_____

_____

_____

P.E.O.P.L.E. GOALS
LEADER PULSE CHECK

Growing your organization takes true leadership. Be an employee advocate and honestly evaluate your behavior. Adjust where necessary and continue what is working well.

Ask yourself: *(List your answers below)*

Am I an employee advocate who prioritizes the employee experience? What am I doing now? What can I do differently?

_____

_____

_____

_____

_____

_____

_____

_____

_____

_____

_____

_____

_____

_____

_____

45

Am I encouraging leaders across the company to make employee engagement a primary goal? What am I doing now? What can I do differently?

_____

_____

_____

_____

_____

_____

_____

_____

_____

_____

_____

_____

_____

_____

_____

_____

_____

_____

_____

_____

_____

_____

Am I allowing leaders and their teams the space to create organically? What am I doing now? What can I do differently?

_____

_____

_____

_____

_____

_____

_____

_____

_____

_____

_____

_____

_____

_____

_____

_____

_____

_____

_____

_____

_____

Am I championing the plan to enhance or design a culture where all employees are thriving? What am I doing now? What can I do differently?

_____

_____

_____

_____

_____

_____

_____

_____

_____

_____

_____

_____

_____

_____

_____

_____

_____

_____

_____

_____

_____

Am I modeling behavior that inspires and engages my organization? What am I doing now? What can I do differently?

_____

_____

_____

_____

_____

_____

_____

_____

_____

_____

_____

_____

_____

_____

_____

_____

_____

_____

_____

_____

_____

_____

_____

Am I empowering employees to perform?
What am I doing now? What can I do differently?

_____

_____

_____

_____

_____

_____

_____

_____

_____

_____

_____

_____

_____

_____

_____

_____

_____

_____

_____

_____

_____

_____

P.E.O.P.L.E. GOALS
QUICK TIPS

- Keep the drive alive in everyone.
- Get to know what you don't know.
- Inspire with originality.
- Actively shape the employee reality.
- Model the behavior for leadership.
- Lead clearly and consistently.

NEXT STEPS

What will you do differently starting today?
*(List your top three next steps along with target
dates and resources needed to accomplish).*

_____

_____

_____

_____

_____

_____

_____

_____

_____

_____

_____

_____

_____

_____

_____

_____

_____

_____

_____

_____

P.E.O.P.L.E. GOALS
10-POINT ORGANIZATIONAL PULSE CHECK

Remember, it all starts with people. Ask employees probing questions to get to real answers and make real progress.

1. I feel connected to my immediate manager.
2. I feel connected to my team.
3. I feel connected to the mission of my company.
4. I feel valued as an employee.
5. I feel challenged in my job.
6. My manager leads in a productive and motivating way.
7. My CEO is connected to what really goes on in our company.
8. My CEO is visible to most employees.
9. Leaders within this organization feel empowered to make decisions.
10. I would recommend my company as a good place to work to my friends and family.

NEXT STEPS

What will you do differently starting today?
(List your top three next steps along with target dates and resources needed to accomplish).

P.E.O.P.L.E. GOALS
SIX QUICK CONNECTORS

Executive leaders may be comfortable in the C-Suite, but the heart of your organization extends further. Plan opportunities to interact with employees at all levels outside of scheduled town halls and employee meetings.

Here are some easy ways to strengthen your connection to employees.

1. Greet employees as you enter the building, elevator, cafeteria, and other common areas.

2. Schedule a daily or weekly walk around to different floors and areas of the company.

3. Arrange informal one-on-one meetings to get to know employees.

4. Plan visits to branch offices.

5. Join a team meeting. (You do not have to stay for the duration).

6. Have lunch with any employee or group of team members.

NEXT STEPS

What will you do differently starting today? *(List your top three next steps along with target dates and resources needed to accomplish).*

_____

_____

_____

_____

_____

_____

_____

_____

_____

_____

_____

_____

_____

_____

_____

_____

_____

_____

_____

_____

_____

_____

TAKEAWAYS FOR PEOPLE LEADERS

My goal is to provide people leaders with insights about what it means to value employees. I emphasize behaviors for us to be mindful of and resolve to start, stop, or continue; where appropriate.

I expressed earlier, this may require you to shift to an employee advocate mindset *to help you engage employees beyond the corner office.* It will take some effort, but it is worth it. Your leadership is required work to connect with your team and set an example for others.

Every leader has a unique style and may be at a different stage in their career and level of responsibility. No matter where you are right now, you must actively invest in ways to accentuate the positive and eliminate the negative during your journey. In doing this, we do not lose ourselves. However, we make progress toward presenting our best selves.

I genuinely hope you use the principles offered in this book to expand your leadership effectiveness.

At the center of all I have shared is that your employees need to know you care about them. As a leader, own how your people experience their time in your company. Commit to doing the work that allows you to *Prioritize, Engage, Originate, Persevere, Lead, and Execute* at your best level.

NOTES

NOTES

_____

_____

_____

_____

_____

_____

_____

_____

_____

_____

_____

_____

_____

_____

_____

_____

_____

_____

_____

_____

_____

_____

_____

_____

NOTES

_____

_____

_____

_____

_____

_____

_____

_____

_____

_____

_____

_____

_____

_____

_____

_____

_____

_____

_____

_____

_____

_____

PAM WESTON

NOTES

 Pam Weston is a senior communications strategist with more than 20 years of experience leading executive communications, internal communications, public relations, and community affairs. As a trusted advisor to C-Suite executives, she has worked with chief executive officers, company presidents, and their teams in several organizations including Fortune 500 companies. Her expertise has guided leaders in industries ranging from financial services to information technology to healthcare, and consumer information solutions.

To arrange speaking engagements, book signings,
and consultations, contact

PamWeston.Blog
PamWestonAuthor@gmail.com

Made in the USA
Columbia, SC
19 June 2022